	DATE DUE		
NOV 23 2004			
2005			
MAR 1 1 2005			
SEP 2 6 2005			
FEB 0 3 2006			
APR 2 1 2006			
AUG 0 8 2007			

Ants

A DENVER MUSEUM
OF NATURE & SCIENCE BOOK

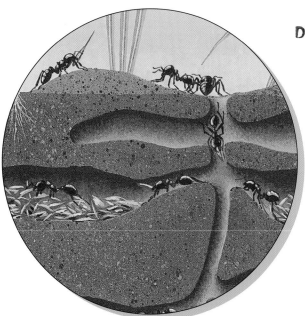

 Written by **Deborah Hodge**
Illustrated by **Julian Mulock**

KIDS CAN PRESS

For Linda Bailey and Cynthia Nugent, two very talented friends

Acknowledgments

I am grateful for the careful review of the art and manuscript by Paula E. Cushing, Ph.D.,
curator of entomology and arachnology, Zoology Department, Denver Museum of Nature & Science, Colorado.
I would also like to thank Heidi Lumberg, former publications director of Denver Museum of Nature & Science Press,
and her staff for their assistance in this project. A special thank you to Julia Naimska for her lovely design
and to my editor, Valerie Wyatt, who makes working on every book fun.

Kids Can Press acknowledges the financial support of the Ontario Arts Council, the Canada Council
for the Arts and the Government of Canada, through the BPIDP, for our publishing activity.
This book is supported in part by the Lloyd David and Carlye Cannon Wattis Foundation.

Published in Canada by
Kids Can Press Ltd.
29 Birch Avenue
Toronto, ON M4V 1E2

Published in the U.S. by
Kids Can Press Ltd.
2250 Military Road
Tonawanda, NY 14150

www.kidscanpress.com

Edited by Valerie Wyatt
Designed by Julia Naimska
Printed in Hong Kong, China, by Sheck Wah Tong Printing Press Limited

The hardcover edition of this book is smyth sewn casebound.
The paperback edition of this book is limp sewn with a drawn-on cover.

CM 04 0 9 8 7 6 5 4 3 2 1
CM PA 04 0 9 8 7 6 5 4 3 2 1

National Library of Canada Cataloguing in Publication Data

Hodge, Deborah
Ants / written by Deborah Hodge ; illustrated by Julian Mulock.

(A Denver Museum of Nature & Science book.)
Includes index.
ISBN 1-55337-066-X (bound).   ISBN 1-55337-655-2 (pbk.)

1. Ants — Juvenile literature. I. Mulock, Julian II. Denver Museum of Nature & Science. III. Title.
IV. Series: Denver Museum of Nature & Science book.

QL568.F7H64 2004   j595.79'6   C2003-902484-9

Photo Credits

Every reasonable effort has been made to trace ownership of and give accurate credit to copyrighted material. Information
that would enable the publisher to correct any discrepancies in future editions would be appreciated.

Abbreviations: t = top; b = bottom; l = left; r = right; c = center

Cover photograph: © Robert and Linda Mitchell

p. 3: (detail) © Mitsuaki Iwago/Minden Pictures; **p. 4:** © Robert and Linda Mitchell; **p. 5:** © Doug Wechsler; **p. 10:** © Robert and Linda Mitchell;
p. 11: © Franz Lanting/Minden Pictures; **p. 15:** © Photospin; **p. 17:** © Mark Moffett/Minden Pictures; **p. 22:** © Mitsuaki Iwago/Minden Pictures;
p. 23: © Robert and Linda Mitchell; **p. 24:** © Paula Cushing; **p. 26:** © Scott Camazine; **p. 27:** © Scott Camazine; **p. 28:** © Joe Warful;
p. 29: © Dr. Laurel D. Hansen, Spokane Falls Community College; **p. 30:** (tl) © Mark Moffett/Minden Pictures; (tr) © Ann and Rob Simpson;
(c) © Robert and Linda Mitchell; (bl) © Robert and Linda Mitchell; (br) © Robert and Linda Mitchell; **p. 31:** (detail) © Doug Wechsler

Kids Can Press is a **Corus**™ Entertainment company

Contents

The Dirt on Ants

What has six legs and can carry many times its own weight? An ant!

Ants can lift heavy objects. This leaf-cutter ant is carrying a leaf that it will chew up and use as fertilizer to grow food.

If you were as strong as an ant, you could lift a grown-up.

Ants are busy insects. They scurry up trees, over rocks and deep underground.

 An Ant

Big **compound eyes** are made up of many smaller parts.

Big **jaws** are used for chewing, digging, carrying and fighting.

Two **antennae** help the ant touch, taste and smell. Ants also "talk" to each other by touching antennae.

The **crop**, inside the abdomen, stores food.

A **stinger** helps this fire ant protect itself. Ants without stingers may bite or spray acid on their enemies.

Hooked **claws** grip well. They let an ant walk upside down.

Build an Ant

Ask an adult to help you make your own ant.

What you need

- 3 Styrofoam balls — 1 large egg-shaped ball; 1 small round ball; 1 medium egg-shaped ball
- black poster paint and a brush
- 1 toothpick
- 3 pipe cleaners
- 2 small paper fasteners for eyes

What you do

1 Paint the balls and toothpick black. Let them dry.

2 Join the balls with a toothpick and pipe cleaner as shown.

3 Push in 6 legs, each made from $\frac{1}{3}$ of a pipe cleaner. Push in 2 smaller pieces of pipe cleaner for the antennae and 2 very small pieces for the jaws.

4 Stick in the paper fasteners for eyes.

What's happening?
An ant is an insect. All insects have six legs and three main body parts: a head, thorax and abdomen.

Head Thorax Abdomen

An ant's long, thin waist lets it twist and turn easily in tight spaces.

9

No Place Like Home

Ants live everywhere in the world, except very cold places. They live in big groups called colonies.

The ants in a colony work together and share food. They dig a home in the soil or make a nest in a log or tree.

A colony of weaver ants makes a nest in a tree. The ants weave leaves together with silky threads made by young ants in the colony.

Some colonies have more than a million ants.

This is an anthill. A colony of ants lives inside. Ants dig tunnels in the earth and use the soil to make an anthill.

Down Under

This colony of harvester ants lives underground. The ants built this nest by digging tunnels and rooms in the dirt.

The colony is hard at work. Every ant has a special job.

This ant is carrying an egg in its strong jaws. Ants move the eggs higher or lower in the nest to keep them at the right temperature.

Harvester ants chew seeds to make a mushy "ant bread" that the colony eats.

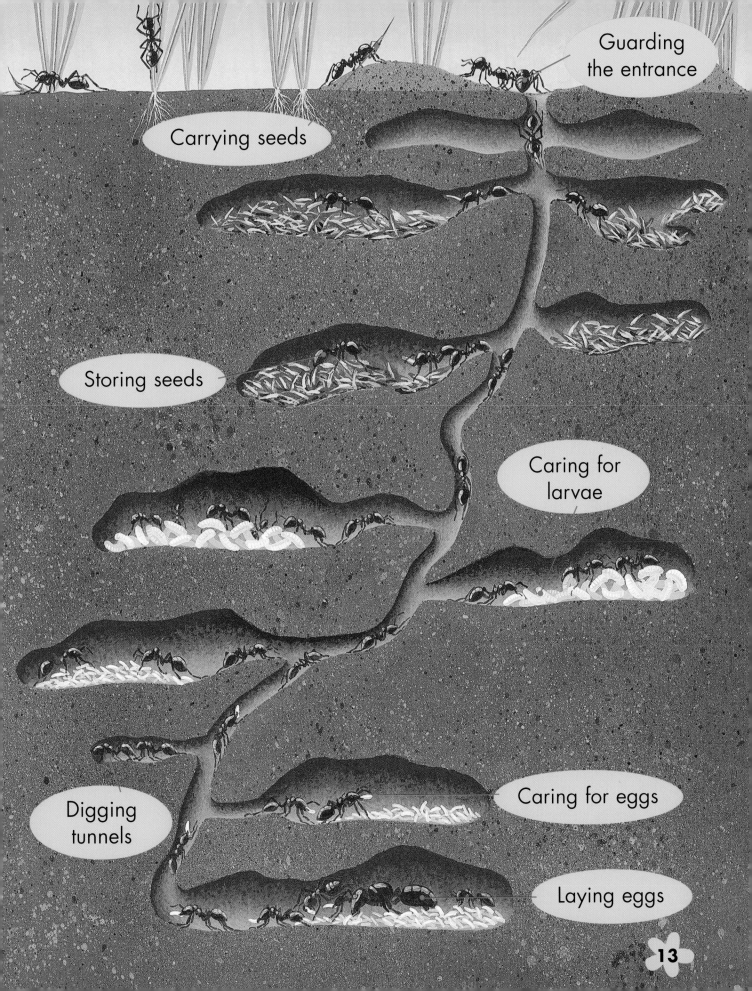

Guarding
the entrance

Carrying seeds

Storing seeds

Caring for
larvae

Digging
tunnels

Caring for eggs

Laying eggs

13

Ants in Action

Ask an adult to help you find some ants
so you can take a closer look.

What you need
- a piece of orange or other cut fruit
- a piece of cookie
- a spoonful of canned chicken, ham or tuna
- 3 small plates
- gardening gloves for anyone handling ants
- glass jar with a lid
- a magnifying glass (optional)

What you do

1 Put one type of food on each plate. Leave the plates near some ants. Wait a while, until the ants find the food. Which food do the ants like?

2 Ask an adult to scoop some food with ants on it into a jar and put on the lid.

3 Look closely at the ants. Use a magnifying glass if you have one. Can you see their three main body parts and their antennae?

4 When you are finished, ask the adult to set the ants free.

What's happening?

Some ants like sweet food. Others like meat or fish. When an ant finds food, it runs to the colony, putting down drops of scent as it goes. Ants from the colony follow this scent trail back to the food.

Don't touch the ants with your bare hands. They may bite or sting you. Avoid fire ants.

Meet the Ants

Three kinds of ants live in a colony: workers, males and a queen.

A **worker** is a female ant. Workers do the day-to-day work of the colony. Most ants are workers. They can live up to a year.

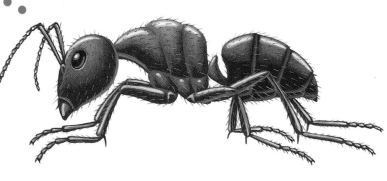

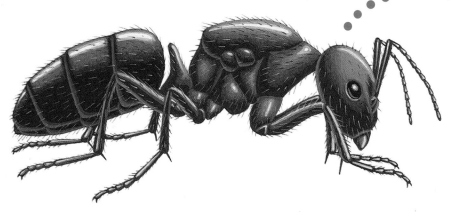

A **queen** lays eggs, which hatch into young ants. Worker ants feed and care for her. Some colonies have more than one queen.

A **male** mates with the queen so she can lay eggs. Male ants die after mating.

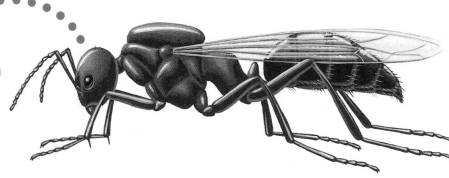

The queen is the biggest ant in the colony. Can you point to her? She is laying eggs.

Some army ant queens lay up to 4 million eggs a year.

Ready, Set, Grow!

An ant grows up in stages. Can you count them? Start with the egg.

1 Egg

An ant begins as a tiny egg. The egg is a little bigger than a grain of sand.

2 Larva

A larva hatches from the egg. Workers feed and care for it. As the larva grows, its skin gets tight. It sheds the skin and grows a new one. This happens four or five times.

3   Pupa

The larva spins a cocoon around its body. Now, it is a pupa. The pupa grows and changes inside the cocoon.

4   Adult

The pupa turns into an adult ant. Workers bite open the cocoon and the pale new ant crawls out. Soon, the ant is strong, dark and ready to work.

Workers lick the eggs and growing ants to keep them clean.

Snug as a Bug

You can make an ant nest out of modeling clay.

What you need
- a shoe box lid
- a pencil
- modeling clay
- glue
- bits of food to make pretend ants: a prune, shredded coconut, rice, puffy rice cereal, light-colored raisins, dark raisins

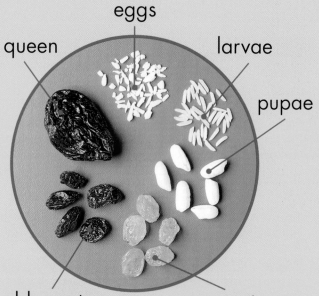

queen
eggs
larvae
pupae
older ants
new ants

What you do

1 Use a pencil to draw 5 small rooms joined by tunnels inside the shoe box lid.

2 Roll long, thin strips of modeling clay. Press the strips along the pencil lines.

3 Glue on pretend ants:
- the prune for the queen and coconut for her eggs
- rice for the larvae
- puffy rice cereal for the pupae
- light raisins for new ants
- dark raisins for older ants

What's happening?
Ants live in different rooms of the nest at different stages of their lives. Workers carry the eggs and larvae to new rooms as they grow.

Hungry Ants

Different ants eat different foods.

Some ants hunt insects. Some ants collect sweet liquid from plants and insects. Still other ants gather seeds or bits of food left by people. The ants carry the food back to the colony.

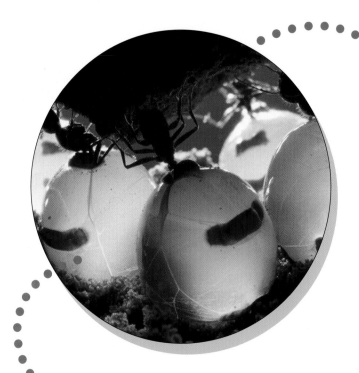

These honeypot ants store sweet liquid in their abdomens. The abdomens stretch like balloons. Later, the ants will bring up the liquid to feed hungry ants in the colony.

Abdomen filled with sweet liquid

Some ants sip sweet liquid from the bodies of tiny insects called aphids.

These hungry ants are attacking a worm. The ants will cut up the worm and carry the pieces back to the colony to eat.

Find the Food!

Pretend you're an ant and try to sniff out some food.

What you need
- a blindfold
- 2 smelly foods (Try a piece of lemon or orange, garlic sausage, strong cheese or peanut butter.)
- 2 smelly nonfoods (Try toothpaste, scented soap, shaving cream or a cotton ball sprayed with perfume.)
- 4 small jars or plastic containers with lids

Ants "smell" with their antennae.

What you do

1 Tie on the blindfold.

2 Ask an adult to put one smelly item in each jar, then put on the lids. There should be 2 foods and 2 nonfoods in the jars.

3 Lift the lid and sniff each jar, one at a time. Can you smell which jars hold food? Can you guess what the food is?

What's happening?

How good was your sniffer? Ants have a very good sense of smell. They use it to find food and get information from other ants. Instead of a nose like yours, ants use their antennae for smelling.

The Ants Go Marching

Army ants don't have homes. They "march" from place to place, hunting for food. The ants cross rivers by floating on leaves or building bridges with their bodies.

Army ants eat everything in their path. These army ants are eating a beetle.

Up to a million army ants travel together.

Army ants cling together in a big ball to rest. The queen, eggs and young ants are protected inside the ball.

Ants in Nature

Ants are important in nature.

Ant tunnels let air into the soil. The air makes the soil healthy and helps plants grow. Ants also get rid of dead plants and insects. And some ants eat pests that harm crops.

This ant is eating a caterpillar that hurts trees.

Ants have lived on Earth for more than 100 million years.

Carpenter ants chew tunnels in fallen logs and other wood. The chewing breaks down the wood and turns it into rich soil.

Other Ants

There are more than 8000 kinds of ants in the world. Here are just a few.

Herdsman ant
carrying an aphid

Giant solitary ant

Conga ant

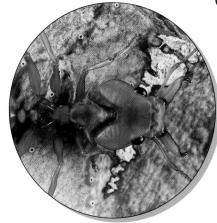

Trap-jawed ant

Asiatic weaver ant

Ant Words

cocoon: a silky covering for a pupa

colony: a group of ants that lives and works together

crop: a pouch inside an ant's abdomen that stores food

larva: the wormlike stage of an ant's life, after it hatches from an egg

male: an ant that mates with the queen

mate: when a queen and male ant come together to produce eggs

nest: a home built by ants, often underground

pupa: the cocoon stage of an ant's life

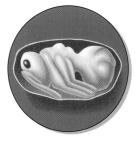

queen: an ant that lays all the eggs in a colony

worker: a female ant that does the day-to-day work of the colony

Index